# Look 3

## A Reading Anthology for Young Learners

LUCY CRICHTON

**NATIONAL GEOGRAPHIC**
**LEARNING**

Australia • Brazil • Mexico • Singapore • United Kingdom • United States

# Contents

# Up in the Air

This is a story about a girl named Mei and her brother, Chen. They're from China. They're in a hot-air balloon competition. Today the wind is very strong. It blows their balloon far away.

Help! Where are we? Is this the U.S.?

Let me look at this map of the world.

4

The balloon blows over a city. It goes near a university.

Excuse me, please! We're lost. We don't know where we are.

Oh! Hello! I'm Professor López. I'm from Spain. Where are you from?

Spain! Oh, that's far away! We're from China.

5

Professor López falls into the basket with Mei and Chen!

We need to get back to China. Can you help us, please?

Yes, of course. Let me see your map ... oops!

Suddenly, the balloon flies off again into the sky. They fly over mountains, rivers, and forests.

Wow! Look at that waterfall!

It's amazing!

The wind blows the balloon up and up. They fly over France, Germany, and Poland.

That's Poland! My aunt and uncle live there. Let's go down and visit them.

They fly down to Warsaw, but they fly too close to the rooftops. Suddenly, they bump into a lot of flags.

Watch out!

At last, they fly through the clouds and see hundreds of hot-air balloons in the sky.

They're near the finish line now. They can hear the judge.
He calls out the winners.

The first prize goes to the balloon with all the flags because it's so international! Congratulations!

FINISH

12

# Arthur the Athlete

Mikael, Simon, Karen, and Staffan are four athletes. They're from Sweden. They're on an adventure race in Ecuador.

The race goes over mountains and through rivers and forests.

First, they stop for something to eat.

There's a dog by the road. He's watching them. He's alone. Poor dog! He looks sad and hungry.

"What's wrong?" Mikael asks.

The dog sits down in front of him and wags his tail. Mikael gives him a meatball. The dog eats it very quickly. He was very hungry!

Mikael pets him. He's a nice dog.
He likes Mikael, too.

Now it's time to go again. There are
miles to go to reach the finish line.

Look! The dog is following them. He wants to go, too! Can he walk that far?

"Go back! Stop following us!" the athletes shout, but the dog doesn't stop. He likes following them.

There's a long way to go. They climb over a mountain.
There's a lot of mud!

Next, they run through a forest. The forest is dark.
They use a compass to find the way.

The dog is right behind them! He's still following them.

He doesn't get tired. He likes running and swimming.
They're almost there now.

After seven days, they reach the finish line. The dog is with them. He's happy and tired.

"This dog is amazing!" they say. "He's brave and strong. He's our faithful friend."

Mikael takes the dog home with him to Sweden.

"I love our new dog! Let's give him a name," they
say. "Let's call him Arthur the athlete!"

Arthur is very happy. He finally has a real home.
He loves his new family!

# The Girl and the Elephant

There are a lot of animals in the world. Some animals are wild, like pandas or elephants. Some animals are pets, like dogs or rabbits.

We can't make wild animals our pets. But this is a very unusual story about a little girl and her special elephant friend.

In central Vietnam, the M'Nong people train wild elephants to work with them. They help the villagers in the fields. This elephant is carrying wood. It's building a house.

The elephants and the villagers spend a lot of time together. They trust each other.

This is Kim Luan. She's watching her father. He's working with the elephants.

"Daddy, do the elephants like helping us?" she asks.

"Yes, they do," he replies. "They're happy near us, but we need to be kind and gentle with them. They're not really pets for children. We always need to respect animals."

Kim Luan is looking at an old elephant in the field. This elephant knows her family very well.

"Can we be friends?" she asks herself.

She walks up to the elephant very slowly and stretches out her hand.

The elephant waves its trunk in the air. It isn't scared. Then
the elephant sniffs Kim Luan's head. This is how elephants
get to know you.

Just then, Kim Luan's mom calls her.

"See you tomorrow!" she whispers to the elephant.

The next day, Kim Luan goes to the elephant.

"I'm going down to the river to get some water. Do you want to come?" she asks.

The elephant follows her down to the river. As they're walking, Kim Luan talks and sings to the elephant.

The little girl and the elephant become very good friends.
Everywhere she goes, the elephant goes, too. Everyone in
the village can see they're friends.

"Let's be friends forever," she says.

# My Tooth Hurts!

It's good to brush your teeth

At least twice a day.

You shouldn't eat a lot of candy,

That's what people say.

Ouch, ouch, ouch!

Something's hurting me.

I think I have a toothache.

I need to look and see.

"You need to see the dentist,"

Mom says in a hurry.

"I'm scared of the dentist,"

But Mom says, "Please don't worry."

We're arriving at the dentist,

I'm feeling hot and cold.

I shouldn't cry, I should be brave,

I should do what I'm told.

There are people in the waiting room,

I'm looking at them all.

Some are short and some are thin,

And some are very tall.

There's a young man sitting next to me,

He has short, dark hair.

The girl over there wearing a pink sweater,

She has curly, blond hair.

Now the nurse is here,

She's looking right at me.

"Pascal Dent," she calls out loud,

"Can you please come with me?"

The dentist says, "Please sit here."

I look at her and see.

She's very nice and gentle.

She's taking care of me.

"Lie back here and let me see

What I can do for you.

It's much quicker than you think,

Only a minute or two."

I open my mouth and she looks in.

She gives a funny cry.

"I can see why your tooth is sore,

I can tell you why!"

"There's a piece of popcorn,

That's why you're feeling pain."

The corn comes out, the dentist smiles.

"Now you're fine again!"


"You should take care of your teeth,

Brush them twice a day.

Be careful eating popcorn,

That's really the best way!"

I'm not scared of the dentist now,

My fears are far away.

I take better care of my teeth

And brush them every day!

# The Legend of the
# Giant's Causeway

This is the legend of the famous Giant's Causeway in Northern Ireland.

A long time ago, there was a giant named Finn McCool. He lived in Ireland with his wife, Oonagh. She was a smart woman, and she loved Finn very much. Finn was tall and strong, and he protected his town and people. Everyone liked him.

One day, Finn decided to walk down by the ocean. Suddenly, a voice shouted, "Hey, McCool! You aren't cool or strong. Why don't you come over here? I can easily beat you in a fight!"

It was the Scottish giant, Benandonner!

Finn didn't like this, so he picked up a big rock. He wanted to throw the rock over the ocean towards Benandonner.

"Did you say I wasn't strong?" he shouted back.

Benandonner just laughed at him.

"Yes, I did! I can't swim, but I'm the strongest giant of them all!"

Finn was so angry that he started to pull rocks off the cliffs and throw them into the water.

"So Benandonner can't swim, huh? Well, I can make a bridge over to Scotland and teach him a lesson."

Finn worked for a week. When he finished the causeway, he shouted over to Benandonner.

"Now you can walk over here and fight me."

The next day, Finn was very tired after lifting all the rocks.

"Oh dear! I'm worried," he said to his wife, Oonagh. "Maybe I'm too weak to fight."

His wife decided to help him.

"Don't worry, my dear. I have a good plan," she said.

She dressed Finn up like a baby, and he climbed into a crib.

When Benandonner arrived later that day, there was a surprise for him!

Benandonner looked closely at the baby. The baby opened its mouth and tried to bite his finger.

Benandonner was scared.

"This baby is so big and so strong his father must be ten times bigger!"

Quick as a flash, he started to run back over the causeway to Scotland. He lifted up the rocks to stop Finn from chasing him. That was the end of Benandonner!

"What a fantastic plan! You really are a very smart woman!" said Finn.

# Roller Coaster Ride

It's summer vacation. Hooray!

My name's Rafaela and this is my brother, André.

We're going to go to an amusement park
near São Paulo. It's called Hopi Hari.

Off we go!

"Are we almost there yet?" I asked after a while.

"No," said Mom. "It's a long way to go. It takes about four hours."

So Dad started to tell us a story.

"The first time I visited an amusement park, your Uncle Jorge got lost!"

"When did you go?" André asked.

"A long time ago," Dad replied. "I was ten and my brother, Jorge, was thirteen. Jorge wanted to go on all the rides, but I was scared. He went on the Ferris wheel. Then he went into the haunted house while I waited for him with my dad."

"After a while, Dad and I started to worry. We didn't know where Jorge was. We didn't have a map, so we decided to go on the mini train around the park to look for him."

"We waited in the line, but when it was our turn to get on, we realized it wasn't the train. It was the roller coaster! There was no way to get off!"

"Wow, Dad! Did you feel scared?" I asked.

"Yes, I did!"

"What did you do?"

"I closed my eyes and we were off! The roller coaster went up and down, and around and around."

"We both screamed really loudly. Everyone in the amusement park looked up at us, including Jorge.

I opened my eyes and saw Jorge far below with some cotton candy. He saw me, too. He was amazed!

Finally, the roller coaster stopped, and Dad and I got off. Jorge asked me if I wanted some of his cotton candy, but I wasn't hungry!"

"That's a really funny story, Dad!" I laughed.

"We're finally here!" Mom said.

"Hooray!"

"Dad," I asked. "Are you going to ride on the roller coaster this time?"

"Of course!" he said. "But please, let's make sure no one gets lost this time!"

"OK, Dad!"

# Activities

**Up in the Air**

**1** **Match.**

Poland   China   Argentina   Japan   Spain   Mexico

1.

3.

5.

2.

4.

6.

**2** **Look at the pictures in Activity 1. Answer.**

**1.** Where's she from? _____ She's from China. _____

**2.** Where's he from? _____

**3.** Where's she from? _____

**4.** Where's she from? _____

**5.** Where's he from? _____

**6.** Where's she from? _____

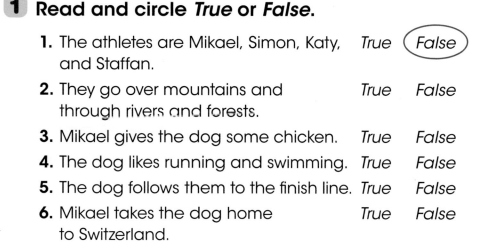

## STORY 2 — Arthur the Athlete

### 1 Read and circle *True* or *False*.

1. The athletes are Mikael, Simon, Katy, and Staffan.   *True*   (*False*)

2. They go over mountains and through rivers and forests.   *True*   *False*

3. Mikael gives the dog some chicken.   *True*   *False*

4. The dog likes running and swimming.   *True*   *False*

5. The dog follows them to the finish line.   *True*   *False*

6. Mikael takes the dog home to Switzerland.   *True*   *False*

### 2 Read and complete.

> forest        ~~There's~~        loves
>
> hungry        running        Arthur the athlete

1. ____There's____ a dog by the road.

2. Poor dog! He looks sad and _____.

3. They run through a _____.

4. The dog likes _____.

5. The dog _____ his new family.

6. Let's call him _____!

59

# STORY 3 The Girl and the Elephant

**1** **Look and circle *is* or *are*.**

1. There *(is)* / *are* an elephant.
2. There *is* / *are* some men.
3. There *is* / *are* a girl.
4. There *is* / *are* a parrot.
5. There *is* / *are* some fish.
6. There *is* / *are* a woman.

**2** **Look at the picture in Activity 1. Read and complete.**

> ~~sitting~~      swimming      drinking
> riding      working      carrying

1. The parrot is _____sitting_____ in a tree.
2. The men are _____ in the field.
3. The girl is _____ an elephant.
4. The elephant is _____ from in the river.
5. The fish are _____ in the river.
6. The woman is _____ a basket.

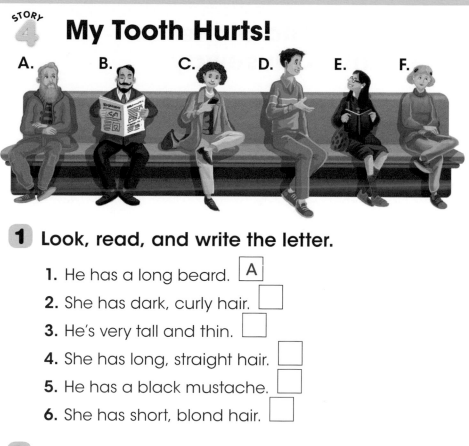

# STORY 4 My Tooth Hurts!

A. B. C. D. E. F.

## 1 Look, read, and write the letter.

**1.** He has a long beard. [A]

**2.** She has dark, curly hair. ☐

**3.** He's very tall and thin. ☐

**4.** She has long, straight hair. ☐

**5.** He has a black mustache. ☐

**6.** She has short, blond hair. ☐

## 2 Read and complete with *should* or *shouldn't*.

**1.** You ____should____ brush your teeth twice a day.

**2.** You _____ eat a lot of candy.

**3.** You _____ be careful when you eat popcorn.

**4.** I _____ be brave.

**5.** I _____ cry.

**6.** You _____ see the dentist when you have a toothache.

# The Legend of the Giant's Causeway

**1** **Order the sentences from 1 to 6.**

**A.** Oonagh dressed Finn up like a baby. ☐

**B.** Finn picked up a big rock to throw into the ocean. ☐

**C.** Finn finished the causeway. ☐

**D.** Benandonner shouted at Finn from over the ocean. ☐

**E.** One day, Finn decided to walk down by the ocean. ☐ 1

**F.** Benandonner started to run back to Scotland. ☐

**2** **Read and answer.**

**1.** Did Benandonner shout at Finn? ___Yes, he did.___

**2.** Did Finn throw a rock into the ocean? _____

**3.** Did Benandonner swim across the ocean? _____

**4.** Did the two giants fight each other? _____

**5.** Did Oonagh have a good plan? _____

**6.** Did Finn chase Benandonner back

to Scotland? _____

# Roller Coaster Ride

## 1 Read and complete.

| were | ~~went~~ | ate | was | went |
|------|------|------|------|------|
| saw | were | went | was | had |

Last weekend, we ¹. ____went____ to an amusement park. It ². _____ so much fun! First, we ³. _____ on the roller coaster. We ⁴. _____ all scared. Next, we decided to go in the haunted house. It ⁵. _____ very dark inside. Then, I ⁶. _____ on the Ferris wheel. I ⁷. _____ my brother far below. After that, we ⁸. _____ all hungry, so we ⁹. _____ some cotton candy. We stayed there until it closed. We ¹⁰. _____ a great time!

## 2 Write about your vacation plans.

This summer, I'm going to _____

Then _____

_____

After that, _____

_____

**NATIONAL GEOGRAPHIC**
**L E A R N I N G**

National Geographic Learning,
a Cengage Company

*Look 3: A Reading Anthology for*
*Young Learners*
**Lucy Crichton**

Publisher: Sherrise Roehr

Executive Editor: Eugenia Corbo

Publishing Consultant: Karen Spiller

Associate Development Editor: Jen Williams-Rapa

Director of Global Marketing: Ian Martin

Heads of Strategic Marketing:

Charlotte Ellis (Europe, Middle East
and Africa)

Kiel Hamm (Asia)

Irina Pereyra (Latin America)

Product Marketing Manager: David Spain

Senior Director of Production: Michael Burggren

Senior Content Project Manager: Nick Ventullo

Media Researchers: Leila Hishmeh, Jeff Millies

Art Director: Brenda Carmichael

Manufacturing Planner: Mary Beth Hennebury

Composition: SPi Global

For permission to use material from this text or product,
submit all requests online at **cengage.com/permissions**
Further permissions questions can be emailed to
**permissionrequest@cengage.com**

ISBN: 978-0-357-02753-0

**National Geographic Learning**
20 Channel Center Street
Boston, MA 02210
USA

Locate your local office at **international.cengage.com/region**

Visit National Geographic Learning online at **ELTNGL.com**
Visit our corporate website at **www.cengage.com**

## Credits

**Cover:** © Brian Skerry/National Geographic Creative.

**Photos: 3** © topseller/Shutterstock.com; **13** © IBL/REX/Shutterstock.com; **14** © Krister Göransson/Peak Performance;
**15** © Krister Göransson/Peak Performance; **16–17** © Krister Göransson/Peak Performance; **18–19** © Krister Göransson/Peak
Performance; **20** © Krister Göransson/Peak Performance; **21** © IBL/REX/Shutterstock.com; **22** © IBL/REX/Shutterstock.com;
**23** © Réhahn Photography; **24** © Claudia Paulussen/Shutterstock.com; **25** © kikujungboy/Shutterstock.com; **26** © Réhahn
Photography; **27** © xuanhuongho/Getty Images; **28** © Réhahn Photography; **29** © Sunphol Sorakul/Getty Images;
**30** © Réhahn Photography; **39** © S-F/Shutterstock.com; **49** © AP Images/Fotoarena.

**Illustrations: 4–12, 58** Ayesha Lopez/Advocate Art; **31–38, 61** Juan Manuel Moreno/MB Artists; **39–48** Adam Horsepool/
Advocate Art; **49–57** CB Canga/Shannon Associates; **60** Teresa Martinez/Astound Art.

Printed in China
Print Number: 08      Print Year: 2024